RENEWING YOUR MIND GOD'S WAY

Renewing Your Mind God's Way

Kenneidra Brown Bender

Contents

Dedication

I give all glory and thanks to my Lord and Savior, Jesus Christ. Through Your calling, I embarked on this incredible journey that stretched me beyond my comfort zone and into a place of purpose. Your guidance has been miraculous, carrying me through moments of uncertainty and challenge—whether in times of doubt, seasons of transition, or stepping into the unknown with only faith to guide me. Without You, this book would not exist.

I also dedicate this to myself—for the perseverance, obedience, and faith required to see this project through. Despite the discomfort and the unchangeable events that arose along the way, I remained steadfast, and this journey has been a testament to my growth. It was not always easy, but it was worth every step.

To those who have walked alongside me—your prayers, encouragement, and unwavering belief in me have meant more than words can express. Thank you for being part of this journey. May this book bless all who read it, as it has been to me in writing it.

Acknowledgments

To my Lord and Savior, Jesus Christ,

For calling me into purpose and guiding me every step of the way.

To my husband, Roc,

For your unwavering love, support, and encouragement. This journey wouldn't have been possible without you by my side.

To my children, Saneidria & Rocquel,

You are my inspiration and joy. Thank you for your patience and for being the heart of everything I do.

To my parents, Kenny & Brina,

Your belief in me, prayers, and sacrifices have shaped me into who I am today. I am forever grateful.

My younger sister, Sakina

I'm thankful for the chance to walk with you as we grew up. Your life has purpose, and God's love for you is tireless. You are always in my heart, and I root for you wherever life's journey takes you.

To my amazing team and closest loved ones,

Thank you for your constant support, prayers, and encouragement during the highs and lows. Your belief in me has made this journey a reality.

To the wisdom of my two grandmothers, Dell & Pearl,

Whose guidance and love continue to shape me, even from heaven. I carry your strength within me, always.

To my older sister, Saneidra, whom I never had the chance to meet,

I know your spirit lives through me; you are forever my angel. Your presence in my life is felt every day.

And to myself,

For the obedience to follow through, even when the road was difficult and uncertain.

This book is a testament to God's perfect timing—it was long awaited but always on His perfect schedule.

Foreword

In a world where so many struggle under the weight of their thoughts, *Renewing Your Mind God's Way* emerges as a profound guide to freedom and transformation. Kenneidra Brown Bender has poured her heart, wisdom, and faith into this devotional, offering a tool for reflection and spiritual renewal.

As a counselor and devoted follower of Christ, Kenneidra has an extraordinary gift for listening to the struggles of those she encounters. Her passion for helping young girls and women navigate life's challenges shines through every page. With grace and clarity, she encourages readers to assess their thoughts and align their beliefs with the truth of God's Word.

Renewing Your Mind God's Way is more than a devotional; it is a transformative experience. Through scripture, reflection, and practical guidance, Kenneidra leads readers to uncover the beauty and strength God has placed within them. Her words challenge us to let go of the lies we've believed and embrace the freedom that comes from trusting in God's promises.

This book is a valuable guide for anyone seeking to live a life anchored in faith and renewed by truth. It reminds us that we are not defined by our doubts or struggles but by God's immeasurable love and purpose for each of us.

As you journey through *Beyond Measure*, prepare to be inspired, challenged, and changed. May this book draw you closer to God and remind you that you are truly beyond measure in Him.

With gratitude,
Dr. Rachel R. Hill, MA, BCMHC, DPS - *Sacred Worx Coaching*

Prologue

Have you ever paused to take inventory of your thoughts? To truly examine the beliefs and patterns that shape your decisions, emotions, and identity? *Renewing Your Mind God's Way* was created from the realization that many of us allow unchecked thoughts to shape our identity, limit our potential, and distort our understanding of God's truth.

As a counselor, I have listened to countless young girls and women share their struggles, each with a unique journey toward healing. They have voiced feelings of inadequacy, confusion, and a longing for purpose. I have seen how negative thought patterns can bind even the most vibrant souls, convincing them that they are less than who God created them to be. But I have also witnessed transformational moments when God's truth replaces the lies, and freedom takes root in their hearts.

This devotional is an extension of my work as a counselor, helping girls and women navigate their struggles, confront limiting beliefs, and embrace the truth of who God created them to be. It is designed to help you examine your thoughts, compare them to God's truth, and allow His Word to bring clarity and renewal. This journey is not about perfection but progress, inviting God into the unfiltered spaces of your thoughts and allowing Him to work.

As you embark on this journey through *Renewing Your Mind God's Way*, know that you are not alone. Each reflection, scripture passage, and exercise is meant to guide you closer to the One who calls you loved, chosen, and redeemed. My prayer is that these pages will illuminate the path toward a life of freedom, faith, and purpose as you learn to see yourself through the eyes of God Almighty.

This is your time to step into a life beyond measure. Let's begin.
— Kenneidra Brown Bender

One

What's in Your Head

Romans 12:2 (NASB) - *And do not be conformed to this world, but be transformed by the renewing of your mind, so that you may prove what the will of God is, that which is good and acceptable and perfect.*

The Mind - *the things you experience and witness are what shape and mold the mind to conduct the thoughts, emotions, and actions throughout life as you know it.*

The Mind - *that which feels, perceives, thinks, wills, and mainly reasons.*

The Bible tells us that we are transformed by renewing our minds so that we can reflect God's will and live in a way that pleases Him without being influenced by worldly desires.

Your mind serves as the guiding force in your life, shaping your path through the thoughts you choose to nurture. Every day, countless thoughts cross your mind, some uplifting, others discouraging. Without examining them, it's easy to let negative thoughts take control. Instead of accepting every thought as truth, take a step back and ask: *Does this align with God's Word?* Filtering your thoughts through

1

His truth allows you to recognize what is real and what is a distortion and whether it stems from false beliefs, cultural influences, or personal insecurities.

Reflections

How do you personally define sanctification, and in what ways does it influence your thoughts, actions, and daily choices?

_____
_____
_____
_____
_____
_____
_____
_____
_____
_____

How important are origins in influencing your future?

_____
_____
_____
_____
_____
_____
_____
_____
_____
_____

Two

Perception Vs. Reality

What do you see in yourself?

Perception is the way we interpret what enters our mind and in Scripture, this is often referred to as *discernment*. Discernment is a spiritual gift given by the Holy Spirit that enables us to distinguish between what is truly real and what only appears to be. However, even our perception of reality can become distorted. Life experiences, emotions, and past wounds can shape how we see things, sometimes causing us to misread situations or people.

That's why it's so important to examine the difference between what is real and what is simply perceived. Understanding the truth of what *did* happen often requires identifying what *did not*. The enemy will try to blur this line, whispering lies that make you question your reality. He'll try to convince you that what you've seen, felt, or lived through isn't valid. That's why discernment is not just helpful—it's essential. It helps you anchor yourself in truth and reject the deceptions that seek to confuse your identity, purpose, and experiences.

Reflections

How do you practice self-awareness in your daily life?

_____
_____
_____
_____
_____
_____
_____
_____
_____
_____

How aware are you of your thoughts, emotions, and mental limits?

_____
_____
_____
_____
_____
_____
_____
_____
_____
_____

Assess Your Assets

2 Corinthians 13:5 (ERV) - *Look closely at yourselves. Test yourselves to see if you are living in the faith. Don't you realize that Christ Jesus is in you? Of course, if you fail the test, He is not in you.*

Assess - *to find out or decide the importance, size, or value of.*

Most people carry themselves in a way that reveals their true character—whether they realize it or not. Others pick up on this through what they observe, sense, or hear in your interactions. The way you engage with people speaks volumes. If you want to better understand your character, start by looking at how you typically act, react, and feel during everyday interactions. Your consistent responses and behaviors shape not only your personality but also how others experience you. And it all starts with your mindset—how you think about yourself and what you believe about your worth deeply influences both your self-perception and how others see you.

The good news is, you don't have to figure all of this out on your own. God knows your thoughts completely—because He created your mind. He walks with you, always. But it's also important to remember that the enemy watches too. He studies your patterns—your words, actions, and behaviors—to find ways to influence or distract you. That's why regular self-reflection is so important. By being intentional about how you respond to situations and how you treat the people God has placed in your life, you guard your mind from being swayed. If your words and behavior consistently reflect the love and character of Christ, you're walking in alignment with His will. But if they don't, it may be a sign that the enemy is trying to steer you off course.

Reflections

What steps do you take to keep your mind open?

_____

_____

_____

_____

_____

_____

_____

_____

_____

_____

What influences your thoughts the most—media, relationships, or personal beliefs?

_____

_____

_____

_____

_____

_____

_____

_____

_____

_____

What's Your Why?

Colossians 3:17 (AMP) - *Whatever you do [no matter what it is] in word or deed, do everything in the name of the Lord Jesus [and in dependence on Him], giving thanks to God the Father through Him.*

Understand- *to accept as a fact or truth or regard as plausible without utter certainty.*

Everything you do has a purpose, often driven by a mix of motivations. Your "why" is deeply connected to the things you've always been passionate about—activities you enjoyed as a child, hobbies you engage in effortlessly, and pursuits you love without expecting anything in return. Understanding these motivations is crucial because they can help you stay focused or regain clarity during challenging times by reminding you why you started in the first place. However, without a clear understanding of your motivation, you may struggle with inconsistency, lose effectiveness, and eventually feel discouraged.

The Bible teaches that the heart and mindset of Jesus Christ should guide everything we do. Seeking God in all things allows us to understand the true intentions behind our desires and actions. Turning to Him helps us avoid falling into the enemy's traps and ensures we remain open to what the Lord is revealing to us. Sometimes, a heartfelt prayer, honest conversation with God, or reflection with Jesus can help resolve misunderstandings and bring clarity. The overwhelming pressure to handle everything on our own can be lifted when we find peace in God, trusting in His revelations and the promises He has spoken over our lives.

Reflections

How well do you know your why? Write it out.

_____

_____

_____

_____

_____

_____

_____

_____

_____

_____

_____

How do you describe yourself?

_____

_____

_____

_____

_____

_____

_____

_____

_____

_____

_____

Transition to Transparency

Psalm 139:23-24 (MSG) - *Investigate my life, O God, find out every-thing about me; Cross-examine and test me, get a clear picture of what I'm about; See for yourself whether I've done anything wrong—then guide me on the road to eternal life.*

Transparent - *free from pretense or deceit.*

True transformation begins with honesty—self-awareness is essential before your perspective can shift. Honesty is crucial in reaching your full potential, as avoiding the truth can create illusions that cloud your judgment and hinder your abilities over time. If being direct and truthful feels uncomfortable, it may be a sign that you're not as open as you believed. Transparency requires courage and confidence but ultimately benefits your mind, heart, and conscience. By embracing honesty, you gain clarity about yourself and unlock the growth needed to reach your full potential.

There is one person and being who is aware of everything you harbor. This deity is all-knowing and quickly sees through the masks you often wear. Even with this, He still died for you to walk shamelessly and not be bound. He knows every choice you make and still decides to extend His grace and mercy. So whenever you have difficulty being honest about yourself, ask God to look within you and assist you in becoming sincere.

Reflection

Have you heard the saying, "You can't fix what you don't see as a problem"? What does it mean to you?

_____

_____

_____

_____

_____

_____

_____

_____

_____

_____

_____

What does it mean to be transparent in your faith and relationships?

_____

_____

_____

_____

_____

_____

_____

_____

_____

_____

_____

Accept Your Accidents

Proverbs 19:8 (AMP) - *He who gains wisdom and good sense loves (preserves) his own soul;*
He who keeps understanding will find good and prosper.

Accept - *to endure without protest or reaction.*

Life inevitably comes with challenges, regardless of how much effort you put into avoiding them. Some of these challenges may be your fault, while others might not be. Either way, they can profoundly impact how you live and interact with the world. These experiences are now part of your life story, and accepting them is the first step toward healing and growth. When you deny or run from the truth, it gains power over you, potentially hindering your progress and keeping you from achieving your desired future. Embracing the reality of your experiences allows you to move forward with intention and resilience.

The challenges you face are far greater than what you can handle alone. From the beginning to the end, the Lord has planned everything purposefully and precisely. God did not create you to live in fear, be consumed by doubt, or remain in denial. Instead, He calls you to walk boldly in faith, trusting that He is in total control and makes no mistakes. Jesus died for your sins and failures long ago so that you can live in freedom today. When you embrace your past as a necessary part of your journey, you move closer to stepping into the future God calls you toward.

Reflections

What type of incidents changed your life?

_____

_____

_____

_____

_____

_____

_____

_____

_____

_____

_____

How can you repent and embrace the next step in your spiritual journey?

_____

_____

_____

_____

_____

_____

_____

_____

_____

_____

_____

Cultivate Clarity

Colossians 4:2-4 (MSG) - *Pray diligently. Stay alert, with your eyes wide open in gratitude. Don't forget to pray for us, that God will open doors for telling the mystery of Christ, even while I'm locked up in this jail. Pray that every time I open my mouth I'll be able to make Christ plain as day to them.*

Clarity - *the quality or state of being clear.*

Clarity is vital in differentiating how you see things from how they truly are. To communicate clearly, you must gain your full intent before relaying the message to yourself or others. Clear communication can ensure that your words are not left behind as an afterthought. Say what you mean and mean what you say; this will create an atmosphere of comprehension. Also, be honest about what you see and feel, and know the difference between that and your potential in all situations, relationships, and emotions. This awareness is essential for healthy communication. Perception without clarity can mislead you unless you seek to ground your reality in truth and transparency.

You are called to speak boldly and not to be timid. Be confident in what you say, as God created you with the Holy Spirit to lead you and your words. If you have anything that needs clarifying, go to God to seek wisdom and know He can use His Word to establish what should be. Although there are things that God meant to leave a mystery to us until we reach Heaven, He is still to be trusted and is knowledgeable so that you may take yourself courageously to Him to gain wisdom to suit your situation better. Persistent prayer with open ears and eyes can ensure the Holy Spirit shows up on your behalf with discernment for your life. So stand firm, dear one, and know your solution is near and awaiting your call.

Reflections

How clearly do you express yourself? Explain.

_____
_____
_____
_____
_____
_____
_____
_____
_____
_____
_____

How clearly do you understand your ultimate goal or desired expectation?

_____
_____
_____
_____
_____
_____
_____
_____
_____
_____
_____

Three

What Are Your Default Settings?

When thinking about the default settings of your mind, the next step is to consider your initial reactions and actions. After evaluating your thoughts to distinguish between what is real and how you perceive it, you must recognize how you respond to situations and events. Reflect on your mindset this morning or as you started your day. Did you approach it with a positive outlook or a negative perspective? How you begin can often influence how things unfold, especially when uninvited thoughts or feelings arise. Look inward and identify the patterns or responses you naturally default to in these moments.

Because sin entered the world through Adam and Eve, it became a part of human nature. We are all born into it. Sin includes anything that goes against the heart and character of the Lord. God's original intention was for your default response to be running to Him, not relying on yourself. Life is full of choices influenced by your emotions, circumstances, and past experiences. So, what will you choose? Matthew 6:33 (AMP) urges you to seek God's character first and foremost. The ultimate goal is to develop Christlikeness as your natural instinct. Achieving this requires constant effort and regular reminders.

Reflections

How do you typically react to unexpected challenges?

_____

_____

_____

_____

_____

_____

_____

_____

_____

_____

_____

In what ways can you look to Jesus' example to be more like Him?

_____

_____

_____

_____

_____

_____

_____

_____

_____

_____

_____

Prevent Pride

Proverbs 29:23 (Voice) - *A person's pride brings him down, but one of humble spirit has a firm hold on honor and respect.*

Toss - *to move with a quick or spirited gesture.*

Pride can be a barrier to growth, relationships, and spiritual maturity. It can often make you believe your way is best or that you can justify your ways because they are more important than others. This idea is damaging to your mind because it can be very misleading. There is no age limit to learning, just as there is no age limit to teaching. Many are willing to lead, but few are open to becoming students. Pride can hinder you from receiving things from others because you want to be in control. You must be willing to listen to others and receive knowledge with respect. But how?

The Bible teaches humility is the key to being lifted in the Lord's eyes, while pride inevitably leads to downfall. Let go of mental barriers caused by making too many excuses, and take responsibility for your actions. In Matthew 16:24-26, Jesus calls His followers to deny themselves, set aside their ego, and follow His ways. This act of surrender is a selfless path to releasing pride and embracing true discipleship.

Reflections

List the habits that reflect and shape your character. Consider daily behaviors, attitudes, and thought patterns that influence how you interact with others and navigate life.

_____
_____
_____
_____
_____
_____
_____
_____
_____
_____
_____
_____

How has pride influenced your decisions or relationships?

_____
_____
_____
_____
_____
_____
_____
_____
_____
_____
_____
_____

Hold on to Humility

Philippians 2:3 - *Don't let selfishness and prideful agendas take over. Embrace true humility, and lift your heads to extend love to others.*

Humility - *freedom from pride or arrogance: the quality or state of being humble.*

After you have torn down the walls of pride, you need a new sense of humility. The commitment to be modest and not allowing your importance to take over your thoughts, feelings, and, most of all, your actions are necessary for the process. Humility is knowing your goals and plans are no more valuable than the next person. Humility could also be reserving your desires for a period to ensure others' happiness. For example, allowing an aching elder to go ahead of you in line, even though you are ready to get home from work, puts a smile on their face. These are all ways you can choose to stay humble on the journey of walking out humility.

Jesus lived the most humble life imaginable, making the ultimate sacrifice by laying down His life for all who had lived and would ever live. Though He was without sin, He faithfully carried out God's assignment. His choice to surrender His life was an act of grace and humility that exemplified His character. Jesus' unwavering commitment to God empowers us to face every challenge with joy and love. Like Jesus, we must remain gracious, even when it hurts or requires us to set aside our pride.

Reflections

What humbling actions can you start taking today?

_____

_____

_____

_____

_____

_____

_____

_____

_____

_____

How will you commit to consistently practicing humility?

_____

_____

_____

_____

_____

_____

_____

_____

_____

_____

Without Worry

Isaiah **41:10** - *Do not be afraid—I am with you! I am your God—let nothing terrify you! I will make you strong and help you; I will protect you and save you.*

Release - *to relieve from something that holds or burdens.*

Worrying can significantly impact your well-being, sometimes even making you physically ill. Negative thoughts can disrupt your hormones, causing them to malfunction and adding to your stress. This cycle of worry has no benefit. The best way to combat it is to shift your focus to things that bring you peace and joy. Concentrating on positive aspects of your life can help ease your stress and reduce the time and energy you spend worrying.

It can be difficult to recognize God's presence, especially if you are searching for a specific sign, word, or confirmation. Yet, you are called to move forward in faith, trusting that the Lord will never lead you astray. God goes before you—not to intimidate, but to guide and protect you. Since He sees and knows all, there is no need to be tense or discouraged. Instead, pursue greatness with confidence, free from anxiety, knowing that the Lord is always with you.

Reflections

How do you personally recognize when God is speaking to you?

_____
_____
_____
_____
_____
_____
_____
_____
_____
_____

How often do you turn to the bible for guidance during stressful times?

_____
_____
_____
_____
_____
_____
_____
_____
_____
_____

Trust the Task

Romans 8:26-28 - *"And the Holy Spirit helps us in our weakness. For example, we don't know what God wants us to pray for. But the Holy Spirit prays for us with groanings that cannot be expressed in words. And the Father who knows all hearts knows what the Spirit is saying, for the Spirit pleads for us believers in harmony with God's own will. And we know that God causes everything to work together for the good of those who love God and are called according to His purpose for them."*

Trust - *firm belief in the character, ability, strength, or truth of someone or something; a person or thing in which confidence is placed.*

You were designed to understand only certain things in life. While you can strive for complete knowledge, achieving it is beyond your purpose. Instead, when you let go of the need to control and trust the more excellent plan, your mind begins to experience freedom. This shift in perspective can even refine or expand your approach, leading to more significant outcomes.

You are never left to navigate life's challenges or uncertainties alone—whether it involves your work, finances, or daily needs. This truth extends to every trouble you may face. God has equipped you with His abundant resources, including the Holy Spirit and the wisdom of those around you, to fulfill the unique plan He has designed for your life. The Spirit intercedes for you, bringing your requests before God and ensuring your needs are heard. You can trust His plan because of His proven faithfulness and unchanging character. God always has His children's best interests at heart, and He is capable and willing to transform any situation for your good. In the end, His purpose for your life will prevail.

Reflections

Have you ever had to accept something that felt uncomfortable or unsettling? If so, how did it influence your life's journey later?

_____

_____

_____

_____

_____

_____

_____

_____

_____

_____

_____

How does trusting God's plan help you navigate uncertainty?

_____

_____

_____

_____

_____

_____

_____

_____

_____

_____

_____

Delete Doubt

Mark 9:21-24 (NLT) - *"How long has this been happening?" Jesus asked the boy's father. He replied, "Since he was a little boy. The spirit often throws him into the fire or into water, trying to kill him. Have mercy on us and help us, if You can." "What do you mean, 'If I can'?" Jesus asked. "Anything is possible if a person believes." The father instantly cried out, "I do believe, but help me overcome my unbelief!"*

Doubt *-Uncertainty, not knowing, not being sure.*

Doubt is a powerful enemy of self-esteem. It undermines confidence and creates obstacles to trusting that things will work out in one's life. To overcome doubt, one must let go of the belief that certain things are "impossible." One can only replace doubt with confidence and hope by embracing faith and possibility.

Belief in Christ is the ultimate way to overcome. Even when unsure, we can trust that the Lord is always indisputable. In fact, He planned the future well before we knew about it. So, our confidence is safest in God because He is the only unchanging and all-knowing God. Allow the Lord to remove doubts from your thoughts and turn them into confidence in Him to make a way.

Reflections

What is the foundation of your confidence—faith, personal achievements, or others' approval?

_____

_____

_____

_____

_____

_____

_____

_____

_____

_____

What are you doubting about God currently?

_____

_____

_____

_____

_____

_____

_____

_____

_____

_____

Have Hope

Isaiah 40:31 - *But those who trust in the Lord will find new strength. They will soar high on wings like eagles. They will run and not grow weary. They will walk and not faint.*

Hope - *to desire something and expect it to happen or be obtained.*

What do you typically think of when it comes to having hope? Take a moment to reflect on this question. Hope often involves setting expectations shaped by the goals we establish. Just as you would set standards for achieving goals, hope also requires a foundational level of assurance or belief to sustain it.

When you place your expectations on people, you open yourself up to disappointment. However, shifting your trust from yourself or others to God — who never makes mistakes — brings more significant benefit to your soul. In times of trials, you can ask Him for renewed strength and let His righteous hand guide and sustain you. He restores what has been depleted and provides the support you need. Choosing to put your hope in God rather than in people invites Him to carry you through difficult times and create a path forward. Trust in the One who will never forsake you.

Reflections

Are you a hopeful person? Why or why not?

_____

_____

_____

_____

_____

_____

_____

_____

_____

_____

_____

What are you currently placing your hope in, and how does it impact your faith journey?

_____

_____

_____

_____

_____

_____

_____

_____

_____

_____

_____

Overcome Fear

Joshua 1:9 (AMP) - *Have I not commanded you? Be strong and coura-geous! Do not be terrified or dismayed (intimidated), for the Lord your God is with you wherever you go.*

Denounce - *PROCLAIM; to announce threateningly.*

Anxiety, stress, and worry are designed to disrupt your mental balance, often leaving you unfocused due to fear of the unknown. However, you have the power to take control of negative thoughts and replace them with positive ones before they escalate into fear and anxiety. By shifting your focus from the "what-ifs" to the "what-is," you release worry and free yourself from overthinking. Let go of the things you can't control and embrace peace by staying present in the moment.

Do not let those who oppose you stir fear within you, for the Lord is with you and goes before you. He invites you to cast your concerns, burdens, and worries upon Him. Fear adds nothing to your life and is a tool of the enemy to distract and weaken you. Remember, the living Word assures us that God is unchanging—He is the same today as He was in the past. This truth is a source of great comfort, as nothing is beyond His understanding or control. Be strong and courageous, trusting that the Lord is with you wherever you go; therefore, you have no reason to fear.

Reflections

How often has fear hindered you from walking by faith?

_____

_____

_____

_____

_____

_____

_____

_____

_____

_____

_____

_____

What situations cause you to overthink, and how do you manage it?

_____

_____

_____

_____

_____

_____

_____

_____

_____

_____

_____

_____

Pray and Obey

Philippians 4:6-7 (AMP) - *Do not be anxious or worried about anything, but in everything [every circumstance and situation] by prayer and petition with thanksgiving, continue to make your [specific] requests known to God. And the peace of God [that peace which reassures the heart, that peace] which transcends all understanding, [that peace which] stands guard over your hearts and your minds in Christ Jesus [is yours].*

Pray - *to make a request in a humble manner; to address God with adoration, confession, thanksgiving, and supplication.*

Obey - *to be obedient; follow instructions.*

Prayer isn't always difficult in itself, but staying focused during prayer can be. It's easy to become distracted, let your mind wander, or slip into routine without truly engaging with God. Real prayer requires humility, vulnerability, and an open heart—it's a sacred conversation with the Lord. But prayer doesn't stop there. Obedience is the next step. Often, after you pray, God will respond with instructions. It's important to be attentive and ready to follow His lead. Both prayer and obedience are essential in deepening your relationship with Him.

Once you've cast out fear and worry, be willing to open your heart to Jesus—and invite Him to open His heart to you. Instead of reacting in frustration when things feel out of your control, pause. Take a breath. Exhale. In that stillness, begin to share your concerns with God. Acknowledge who He is, and He will meet you there with peace. From that place, follow the direction He gives. In every trial, understanding the power of both *praying* and *obeying* is vital. Together, they strengthen your faith and align your heart with His will.

Reflections

What does your prayer posture and position look like?

_____

_____

_____

_____

_____

_____

_____

_____

_____

_____

_____

_____

How often do you intentionally pause to listen for God's voice during prayer?

_____

_____

_____

_____

_____

_____

_____

_____

_____

_____

_____

_____

Four

Renewing Your Mind

Renewing your mind requires vulnerability and relinquishing old ways, thoughts, and patterns. It can be thought of as a detox or deep cleaning process that begins with clearing out the old to make room for the new. Often, this requires discipline to make the necessary changes. First, you must believe that forming new habits is possible. Restoration is the end goal.

Through Christ, you are allowed to be renewed. Renewal is not based on your past, present, or the uncertainty of the future. The Lord loves you as His child so much that He gave His only begotten Son so that He would die to cover every sinful thing that was and is to come. This means that once you confess Him as Lord and Savior and go into a relationship with Him, you have permitted to be renewed spiritually and holistically. The journey is not always easy, but it sure is worth the end result of eternal life with the Lord and joy and peace on this earth.

Reflections

If you could reset your mindset, what new thought patterns would you cultivate?

_____

_____

_____

_____

_____

_____

_____

_____

_____

_____

_____

Make a list of the areas where you're asking the Lord for renewal and restoration. Take time to pray over each one and reflect on what God may be revealing to you.

_____

_____

_____

_____

_____

_____

_____

_____

_____

_____

_____

Master Your Mind

Psalm 51:10 - *"Create in me a new, clean heart, O God, filled with clean thoughts and right desires."*

Recreate - *to give new life or freshness to.*

As you grow and evolve, your mind must be renewed to match each new season of your life. Staying the same is not an option. Just as your physical body constantly replaces old cells with new ones, your mind, heart, and spirit also need regular renewal, no matter what life brings. This spiritual clearing is essential for transformation. By intentionally releasing old thoughts and habits, you open yourself up to new growth and a better version of yourself.

Scripture calls us to cleanse our souls. This begins in the mind, where you surrender your old ways and past desires to the Lord. When you choose to follow Christ, you invite Him to wash you clean through His Spirit. This act of surrender marks the beginning of your transformation. In Christ, you become a new creation, made alive with fresh purpose. Renewing your mind God's way means allowing Him full access and not just to your thoughts, but to your entire life. It's a journey of letting go, so He can lead you into something greater.

.

Reflections

When you pray, do you sense that God speaks to you? If so, how frequently?

_____

_____

_____

_____

_____

_____

_____

_____

_____

_____

_____

How does worry affect your prayer life, and how can you shift from fear to faith?

_____

_____

_____

_____

_____

_____

_____

_____

_____

_____

_____

_____

Force Forgiveness

Colossians 3:13 (TLB) - *Be gentle and ready to forgive; never hold grudges. Remember, the Lord forgave you, so you must forgive others.*

Force - *to break open or through.*

Sometimes, the things we need most are the hardest to do. Having a necessary but uncomfortable conversation, for example, often gets pushed to the bottom of our to-do list even when we know it could lead to healing. It's not always easy to confront those who have hurt us or to take steps toward reconciliation. In fact, trying to make peace can sometimes stir up more emotions, raise new questions, or even open old wounds.

And here's the truth: what feels like a clear offense to you might not even register to the other person. They may not see or acknowledge any wrongdoing at all. That's why forgiveness can't depend on someone else's apology or understanding. Forgiveness is not for *them*—it's for *you*.

Just as the Lord forgives us, we must be willing to confront the unforgiveness in our own hearts. It's not easy, but peace begins when we surrender the need for revenge and trust God to handle what only He can. When you choose forgiveness, you break the chains that have kept you stuck in pain. And on the other side of that release, you may find unexpected freedom, healing, and breakthrough. Forgiveness is more than a choice—it's a reflection of God's heart in you.

Reflections

What steps are you taking to overcome unforgiveness?

_____

_____

_____

_____

_____

_____

_____

_____

_____

_____

_____

In what ways do you notice resentment in your life?

_____

_____

_____

_____

_____

_____

_____

_____

_____

_____

_____

Pure Pores

1 John 1:9 (AMP) - *If we [freely] admit that we have sinned and confess our sins, He is faithful and just [true to His own nature and promises], and will forgive our sins and cleanse us continually from all unrighteousness [our wrongdoing, everything not in conformity with His will and purpose].*

Purify - *to grow or become pure or clean.*

Just as most stores and businesses do a clearance when the seasons change, this is also a good tool to use in life. When preparing for the next season, there is plenty of need to clean your mind before taking in anything new. Preparation is a way to brace for growth. It is not harboring things that have taken up space and not benefited you. It calls for you to recognize the thoughts and clutter that are not beneficial for the future.

With all things considered, the purification process is anything but easy for a person. You need the Lord to lead and guide this journey to produce long-term results. All things are possible with Him, even if something has been there for years and left a scar. With the dying of Christ on the cross, we all have the opportunity to be purified by accepting Jesus as our Savior. This purification is for the whole person, mind, heart, spirit, and soul. Allow God to move and know He has the power to clean and clear any and all stains from your mind.

Reflections

When was the last time you cleared your mind of mental clutter—and what impact did it have on your thoughts, emotions, or spiritual clarity?

_____
_____
_____
_____
_____
_____
_____
_____
_____
_____
_____

How would you describe your personal growth journey right now?

_____
_____
_____
_____
_____
_____
_____
_____
_____
_____
_____

Extend Empathy

1 Corinthians 15:10 - *But whatever I am now, it is all because God poured out such kindness and grace upon me—and not without results: for I have worked harder than all the other apostles, yet actually I wasn't doing it, but God working in me, to bless me.*

Hebrews 12:11 - *Being punished isn't enjoyable while it is happening—it hurts! But afterward, we can see the result: a quiet growth in grace and character.*

Extend - to make the offer of; to make available.

Grace - approval, favor; mercy, pardon.

Have you ever gained something you knew you were undeserving of? Have you ever gotten away with something you knew was a punishable offense? Those are examples of grace. They are often unrecognized in our lives. Whether it is a waived fee, a dismissed ticket, or even an accident you almost had, grace leads you through.

It is your job to make that same mercy available to others even when you think they do not deserve it because none of us do. Showing mercy should be done without regard to the other person earning it because if it were not for God's grace in the first place, you would have to pay for the sins you were born into without prejudice. Sharing God's grace is a humble act that the Lord smiles upon. This act of extending grace shows Him that it is not about you but the love He showed us through His son, Jesus Christ. Grace is an act of selflessness.

Reflections

What does grace look like in your life?

_____

_____

_____

_____

_____

_____

_____

_____

_____

_____

What are you giving away freely—through your words, actions, or attitude—that does not reflectGod'ss heart, and why do you think that is?

_____

_____

_____

_____

_____

_____

_____

_____

_____

_____

Train Your Thoughts

Philippians 4:8 - *And now, dear brothers and sisters, one final thing. Fix your thoughts on what is true, and honorable, and right, and pure, and lovely, and admirable. Think about things that are excellent and worthy of praise.*

Train - to direct the growth of (a plant) usually by bending, pruning, and tying; to teach in an art, profession, or trade; to teach (an animal) to obey; to make ready for a test of skill or strength; to aim at an object or target.

Your mind is an operation center for the rest of the body. How it functions directly affects how the body responds. Therefore, it is vital to monitor the content entering and roaming freely inside your mind. Caring for your thoughts and guarding your mind is maintenance and treatment for managing those thoughts.

What we choose to think about, watch, and listen to directly impacts how we live. What we take from situations, good or bad, positive or negative, tells our body, mind, or heart what to do next with it. When we allow ourselves to be consumed with malicious thoughts, we are allowing ourselves to be vulnerable to doing wrong, hurt, pain, and more. We have to guard our hearts as Philippians 4:7 says, along with the mind, through Christ. We must remember to give God the glory in everything, and He will work it all together. Meditate on His word, trust His power, and know that God will make perfect peace in each situation.

Reflections

Who or what has the most influence over your thoughts right now?

_____

_____

_____

_____

_____

_____

_____

_____

_____

_____

How are your thoughts influencing your choices?

_____

_____

_____

_____

_____

_____

_____

_____

_____

_____

Develop Discipline
Through Fasting

Matthew 4:4 - *But Jesus told him, "No! The Scriptures say, 'People do not live by bread alone, but by every word that comes from the mouth of God.*

Discipline - to train or develop through instruction and exercise especially self-control.

Fasting - to abstain from food; to eat sparingly or abstain from some foods.

God instills desires in our hearts with purpose, yet we often attempt to fulfill them through our own reasoning rather than seeking His guidance. While food may seem like an easy solution for comfort or discipline, we must learn to trust God and seek His guidance on when and how to fast. His timing and path may not always be our first choice, but obedience to Him is key. These practices teach us patience, strengthen our faith, and cultivate spiritual endurance. Through fasting, we learn to deny ourselves and focus on God. Prayer deepens our relationship with Him, and studying His Word equips us with wisdom and guidance for our journey.

It's important to consult God in all decisions, as not every opportunity is from Him. More money, better benefits, or an easy "yes" may seem like blessings, but they can sometimes be distractions meant to pull you away from His plan. Many struggle with obedience, avoiding jobs with lower wages, fewer benefits, or ministry-focused positions—fearing sacrifice—when these opportunities might provide the time and space needed to align with His Word and purpose. Honoring Christ should take priority over conforming to the world's standards. The only way to confidently walk in God's will is to wait on Him, practice discernment, and embrace regular seasons of fasting. True obedience requires a willingness to follow Christ wherever and however He leads, with discipline and trust.

Practically, this means preparing yourself before a fast. Set aside intentional time with God to strengthen your relationship with Him. Create a plan that includes prayer, studying His Word, and seeking clarity on what He calls you to sacrifice in this season. If you feel the need to fast but are unsure of the details, use this time to seek God's direction. When you put Him first, He will align everything else for your good.

Reflections

What are some goals of your fast(s)?

_____

_____

_____

_____

_____

_____

_____

_____

_____

_____

_____

How do you plan to use your time of fasting wisely?

_____

_____

_____

_____

_____

_____

_____

_____

_____

_____

_____

Positive Prayer

1 Thessalonians 5:16-18 (MSG) - *Be cheerful no matter what; pray all the time; thank God no matter what happens. This is the way God wants you who belong to Christ Jesus to live.*

Positive - fully assured; CONFIDENT.

Stay cheerful, pray consistently, and thank God no matter the results. As a Christian, you are told to do this.

Sample Prayer:
Lord, thank you for my joyful spirit. I appreciate my ability to be positive in the midst of this situation. I ask for forgiveness for not speaking to you first. I have realized that bringing things to You first will lead to better solutions than trying to steer my own mind, especially when I need guidance on a concern. Change my mind and heart and how I handle them in the future.

You must not get caught up in pleading in your prayer time. Prayers should first be led by adoration, confession of sins, and thanks for what the Lord has done before soliciting new things. I was taught to think of the acronym ACTS. This prayer format can be followed by always keeping a grateful heart and finding joy in all situations. Remember, someone always wishes they were where you are, so be grateful and remain positive to keep yourself from complaining.

Reflections

Write down words, thoughts, or things that make you feel encouraged, joyful, or uplifted.

_____
_____
_____
_____
_____
_____
_____
_____
_____
_____
_____
_____

Do you believe prayer is a key to Christianity? If so, why?

_____
_____
_____
_____
_____
_____
_____
_____
_____
_____
_____
_____

Welcome Worship

Psalm 100:2 - *Worship the Lord with gladness; come before him with joyful songs.*

Worship - to regard with great or extravagant respect, honor, or devotion.

What does your waiting look like? Is it worrying? Is it sitting anxiously? Do you feel overwhelmed? Worship welcomes you into God's presence, where there is liberty. You are to take your focus off the things that could be and remain in Him for the things with a joyful heart. Heartfelt worship also allows you to show reverence to the One and Only who can make a difference in your situation, even when you cannot.

The Word welcomes you into communion with God, inviting you to dwell with Him. There is no need to be afraid in this space. God is the Anchor and Lord of all situations. Nothing catches Him by surprise. He invites you to spend time with Him throughout your day, whether through a song, a sermon, or even a message you see on a car tag. When these moments arise, reflect and give God glory and the highest praises.

Reflections

How can you add worship into your daily life?

_____
_____
_____
_____
_____
_____
_____
_____
_____
_____

What are some benefits of worship?

_____
_____
_____
_____
_____
_____
_____
_____
_____
_____

Speak Strength

Mark 9:17-29 - *A man in the crowd answered, "Teacher, I brought you my son, who is possessed by a spirit that has robbed him of speech. Whenever it seizes him, it throws him to the ground. He foams at the mouth, gnashes his teeth, and becomes rigid. I asked your disciples to drive out the spirit, but they could not. "You unbelieving generation," Jesus replied, "how long shall I stay with you? How long shall I put up with you? Bring the boy to Me." So they brought him. When the spirit saw Jesus, it immediately threw the boy into a convulsion. He fell to the ground and rolled around, foaming at the mouth. Jesus asked the boy's father, "How long has he been like this?" "From childhood," he answered. "It has often thrown him into fire or water to kill him. But if you can do anything, take pity on us and help us." "'If you can't?" said Jesus. "Everything is possible for one who believes." Immediately the boy's father exclaimed, "I do believe; help me overcome my unbelief!" When Jesus saw that a crowd was running to the scene, he rebuked the impure spirit. "You deaf and mute spirit," he said, "I command you, come out of him and never enter him again."*

Speak - to express orally; declare.

Power - of, relating to, or utilizing strength; POWERFUL.

Not every struggle we face as God's children is ours to fix in the physical. Some situations are divine assignments meant to go directly to God. He alone has the power to shine light on the hidden parts and get to the root of what's going on. Just like in the referenced scripture, I carried unresolved pain, emotions, and memories in my spirit since childhood. For a long time, I bore it alone—until my confidence in God grew strong enough to confront it.

Shame and guilt no longer had the authority to throw me into the fire and consume me. I began to take responsibility for my flaws and failures—not to stay stuck in them, but to let God cleanse and renew me. It wasn't enough to pretend things were okay. I had to learn to *discern* what was truly happening and *speak* against the lies and spiritual attacks that threatened to destroy my mind, my marriage, my peace, and my purpose.

My breakthrough came when I chose to trust the power of God at work in me. I realized that with Him, I could do more than survive—I could speak life and declare freedom. Some things can *only* be broken through prayer and deep relationship with God. I've learned to trust that He sees it all, and I've discovered that there is *power in my voice*—a power that just needs to be activated.

Speech is a divine gift—not everyone has it, which makes it all the more sacred. It's not just about talking; it's about speaking with wisdom, purpose, and faith. According to Romans 1:16, the power of salvation is available through Jesus Christ to those who believe. But to truly awaken that power within, we must be willing to *speak boldly* about the truth.

If you only think it but never say it, your belief may remain hidden and powerless. Why? Because life and death are in the power of the tongue (Proverbs 18:21). The spoken word builds belief. What you speak over yourself matters. Speak strength. Speak truth. Speak life.

Reflections

How can you improve the things you are speaking about over your life?

_____

_____

_____

_____

_____

_____

_____

_____

_____

_____

Where do you invest most of your time, energy, and spiritual focus?

_____

_____

_____

_____

_____

_____

_____

_____

_____

_____

Profess His Promises

Psalm 145 - *I will exalt you, my God, the King; I will praise Your name for ever and ever. Every day I will praise You and extol Your name for ever and ever. Great is the Lord and most worthy of praise; His greatness no one can fathom. One generation commends Your works to another; they tell of Your mighty acts. They speak of the glorious splendor of Your majesty— and I will meditate on Your wonderful works. They tell of the power of Your awesome works— and I will proclaim Your great deeds. They celebrate Your abundant goodness and joyfully sing of Your righteousness. The Lord is gracious and compassionate, slow to anger, and rich in love. The Lord is good to all; He has compassion on all He has made. All Your works praise You, Lord; Your faithful people extol you. They tell of the glory of Your kingdom and speak of Your might, so that all people may know of Your mighty acts and the glorious splendor of Your kingdom. Your kingdom is an everlasting kingdom, and Your dominion endures through all generations. The Lord is trustworthy in all He promises and faithful in all He does. The Lord upholds all who fall and lifts up all who are bowed down. The eyes of all look to You, and You give them their food at the proper time. You open Your hand and satisfy the desires of every living thing. The Lord is righteous in all His ways and faithful in all He does. The Lord is near to all who call on Him, to all who call on Him in truth. He fulfills the desires of those who fear Him; He hears their cry and saves them. The Lord watches over all who love Him, but all the wicked He will destroy. My mouth will speak praise of the Lord. Let every creature praise His holy name for ever and ever.*

Profess - to declare or admit openly or freely; affirm.

Negative thoughts often rush in without hesitation. They don't need our permission and certainly don't wait for us to speak them out loud. They show up uninvited. But just because a thought enters our mind doesn't mean we must accept it. We have the power—through Christ—to either receive or reject what doesn't align with truth.

Sometimes, when negativity or spiritual attacks arise, we're not only allowed but *called* to cancel them out with the Word of God. Whether through scripture, worship, praise, or simply declaring God's goodness, we have weapons to resist the enemy's lies. We will face hardships because of the Fall and the reality of sin. But our response matters. One of the most powerful things you can do is open your mouth and fill the atmosphere with gratitude. Speak life. Speak praise. Even when your circumstances don't feel good, the Lord *is* good—and He desires to renew your mind, restore your heart, and strengthen your spirit.

Keep a heart that honors God. No matter what life looks like, His faithfulness never wavers. The truth is God's goodness will always outweigh the darkness. So don't be discouraged—be anchored.

Ask yourself: *Are you in agreement with God?* What declarations are you making about your life? The promises of God are "Yes" and "Amen" (2 Corinthians 1:20). But we must not forget to *declare* those promises—out loud and with belief. It's one thing to read them, but it's another to *believe them for yourself* and walk in that truth.

Hebrews 4:12 reminds us that the Word is alive and active. That means what God has spoken is still working today. Train your tongue to speak what God has already said about you. Speak it boldly, speak it often, and speak it with faith.

Reflections

What are some of God's promises in the Bible that you can declare over yourself as truth?

_____

_____

_____

_____

_____

_____

_____

_____

_____

_____

How can you receive what has been promised to you by inheritance from Our Father God?

_____

_____

_____

_____

_____

_____

_____

_____

_____

_____

Believe You Can Achieve

Matthew 21:22 - *"If you believe, you will receive whatever you ask for in prayer."*

Believe - to have a firm conviction as to the goodness, efficacy, or ability of something.

Before embracing change, we must first believe that transformation is possible. We have to decide in our minds that our situations can shift to become better. As we take on Godly things, let us have faith in Christ. We must grasp the concept of how we can believe in the power of God to swivel situations for us. Belief allows us to walk boldly in His blessings. We must not doubt but instead trust in the Word of God to assist us in achieving the next blessing available.

Faith in the Father is fruitful. Your future follows the faith-filled life you have right now. Take time and journal what you believe God will do in your life. This will allow you to date and go back to remember these answers to prayers that will strengthen your future faith even more because you will be able to say, "If He did it before, He can do it again!" Trust God to be the God He is, was, and always will be.

Reflections

What core beliefs influence how you see yourself and the world?

_____

_____

_____

_____

_____

_____

_____

_____

_____

_____

_____

List some things you would like to achieve this season/year.

_____

_____

_____

_____

_____

_____

_____

_____

_____

_____

_____

Persevere Purposefully

James 1:12 - *Blessed is the one who perseveres under trial because, having stood the test, that person will receive the crown of life that the Lord has promised to those who love Him.*

Persevere - to persist in a state, enterprise, or undertaking in spite of counter influences, opposition, or discouragement.

Some of our most significant tests are our most considerable testimonies. The trials we encounter are not always meant nor sent to harm us. God can still get the glory from our affliction. I believe God allows us to be placed in the fire sometimes so that we will be reminded that we need Him. We often realize the power only His Hand can show amid our struggles. We must choose to stay the course and be determined to persist no matter what it looks like. This beauty is Jehovah's mighty hand-print in the fire with us that turns pressure into the pruning of our plans and purposes. God is so intentional. He has forever wanted us to have an everlasting life and has made several ways to ensure we can obtain it. *I am thankful for my crown.*

Someone once asked me if I remembered why I started seeking God more. This required me to recall my "why," which was revealed to me by the Lord as I matured spiritually. You also need to know what it means for you to move forward on purpose. No matter what obstacles you face, continue to push through. Remember your reason and know that what doesn't kill you will strengthen you. For as long as you are living, you are full of purpose - so leave here empty with your purpose fulfilled in whatever areas God leads you!

Reflections

In what ways can you persevere despite your circumstances?

_____
_____
_____
_____
_____
_____
_____
_____
_____
_____

What do you believe is your God-given purpose, and how are you pursuing it?

_____
_____
_____
_____
_____
_____
_____
_____
_____
_____

Five

The Mind of Christ

1 Corinthians 2:16 - *for, "Who has known the mind of the Lord so as to instruct him?" But we have the mind of Christ.*

2 Corinthians 1:21 - *Now it is God who makes both us and you stand firm in Christ. He anointed us.*

As 2 Thessalonians 1:11 reminds us, we should remain focused on Jesus in prayer, striving to fulfill His unique calling. This focus involves seeking to have the mind of Christ, embodying His love, and serving as His hands and feet on Earth. Growing in relationship with Him means learning His heart and aligning our desires with His. As we go about our daily lives, keeping His will in our minds ensures that our thoughts and actions increasingly reflect His nature. This process requires openness, vulnerability, and faith, allowing the Holy Spirit to guide our steps. With the mind of Christ, we understand that it is through His sacrifice that we live, breathe, and find our purpose. Therefore, we are called to remember Him and let His presence shine through everything we do.

Reflections

What does the Bible say about the mind of Jesus Christ?

_____

_____

_____

_____

_____

_____

_____

_____

_____

_____

Why must you align your thoughts and mindset with the Mind of Christ? How does adopting His perspective influence your decisions, attitudes, and spiritual growth?

_____

_____

_____

_____

_____

_____

_____

_____

_____

_____

_____

_____

Give Honor to God

Ezra 10:11 - *Now honor the Lord, the God of your ancestors, and do His will. Separate yourselves from the people around you and from your foreign wives.*

Honor - to regard or treat with admiration & respect; to regard or treat with honor

You must revere the Lord first and foremost before pursuing things on a list or in your routine. Lead with love, which is what "honor" translates to in the Bible and is spoken of often. The Lord loves you with everything and wants you to withhold nothing in returning that same love. Seeking Him and all that pleases Him is a huge way to show respect and honor to Him. Giving glory to God in all you do exalts Him and shows admiration towards His grace and mercy for your life. This is the least that can be done for Him, who sent His only begotten Son to die for your sins (John 3:16).

This looks like practically thanking God at the beginning of your day for the simple things, turning to Him when faced with decisions, and pondering what will make Him happy. Praying and staying in communication are relationship strengths, as well as reading His Word. Release anything that can clog your spiritual ears from hearing Him, including grudges and unforgiveness. Last, praise God to give Him glory and commend Him for all He's done. The Lord loves to be exalted as the One and Only mighty God. Love Him and receive His love in return.

Reflections

Name things, people, and places you currently honor.

_____

_____

_____

_____

_____

_____

_____

_____

_____

_____

Who is God to you? What does He mean to you?

_____

_____

_____

_____

_____

_____

_____

_____

_____

_____

Rest in Refuge

Psalm 91:9-11 - *If you say, "The Lord is my refuge," and you make the Most High your dwelling, no harm will overtake you, no disaster will come near your tent. For He will command His angels concerning you to guard you in all your ways; "Because he loves Me," says the Lord, "I will rescue him; I will protect him, for he acknowledges my name. He will call on Me, and I will answer him; I will be with him in trouble; I will deliver him and honor him. With long life, I will satisfy him and show him My salvation."*

Refuge - shelter or protection from danger or distress.

Many people are not born into a safe or stable home, let alone one that provides comfort for children. Like myself, some were born into a stable environment and soon after lost it due to unforeseen circumstances, so things went from good to bad before our eyes. God has told us that we have protection and safety in Him, so we must learn to dwell in Him along the way, no matter what that looks like. He has formed a shelter in Him that walks us through the things that cause our anxiety to rise. Christ challenges us to put our faith in Him as we allow God's angels to work around us and be messengers of His Word. All we need to do is seek God and rest in His Word. *Thank you for the protection you have given, Lord. Even in tough times, you will deliver us.* He rescues us from condemnation and extends salvation.

Oftentimes, this physically means to walk away. This could be from a dangerous situation; this could mean abuse, hurt, stress/strain, and even idols. Those things that hinder us from hearing and doing right by God and what we know pleases Him are necessary to let go of and bring under God's coverage. It is not about how others see us and what we do when others look; what are you doing when no one can see you? This may mean walking away from familiar places, people, and habits, including your comfort zones. None of this is easy because they are led by fear and pain – and it is never easy to walk away, but it is worth consulting God to see what His plan is and what will bring you peace. The amount of peace the Lord gives cannot be replaced by anything, especially something holding you back from being all in for God. God wants you to desire Him and be afraid to lose Him as much as you fear losing what you do not want to let go of.

Reflections

How often and in what ways do you rest in Him?

_____

_____

_____

_____

_____

_____

_____

_____

_____

_____

What do you rely on for security, comfort, or protection? Are you seeking refuge in God, or are there other things you tend to depend on?

_____

_____

_____

_____

_____

_____

_____

_____

_____

_____

Surrender Your Soul

Genesis 45:4-11 (MSG) - *"Come closer to me," Joseph said to his brothers. They came closer. "I am Joseph, your brother whom you sold into Egypt. But don't feel bad, don't blame yourselves for selling me. God was behind it. God sent me here ahead of you to save lives. There has been famine in the land for two years now; the famine will continue for five more years — neither plowing nor harvesting. God sent me ahead to pave the way and make sure there was a remnant in the land to save your lives in an amazing act of deliverance. So you see, it wasn't you who sent me here but God. He set me in place as a father to Pharaoh, put me in charge of his personal affairs, and made me ruler of all Egypt. "Hurry back to my father. Tell him, 'Your son Joseph says: I'm master of all of Egypt. Come as fast as you can and join me here. I'll give you a place to live in Goshen where you'll be close to me — you, your children, your grandchildren, your flocks, your herds, and anything else you can think of. I'll take care of you there completely. There are still five more years of famine ahead; I'll make sure all your needs are taken care of, you and everyone connected with you — you won't want for anything.'*

Surrender - the giving of oneself or something into the power of another person or thing.

Soul - a person's total self, classified as the mind, will, and emotions.

Sometimes, it may seem like God forgot about us, but that is impossible because of who He is. We are His, created for such a time as this. We must remain confident in the Lord that He is always thinking of us. His help is sufficient, just like His grace. Be assured that if God tells you to do something, the Creator will bless it, not only for you but also for your legacy and those to come.

Because God is so good, He can flip an entire plan of the enemy. The evil will not deter his plan for us pushed upon us. He will ensure His ultimate plan is met. He uses the enemy's actions to better us. In my case, I was sent here to help save multiple lives for the goodness of God. So that is what I shall do through submission to Him. With God's help, I will walk this new path despite the pandemic and other global impacts we have had to take place. *Many will be delivered, and all connected to me will be blessed by my obedience. I trust the Lord, not the fleshly and earthly things. I am confident that Jehovah Jireh will provide, even in the hard times.* He is loyal to His Word and will never lie. He didn't say it would be easy, but He said He would never forsake us and always take care of us. Look to Him and trust Him along the way.

Reflections

What are the things or people you prioritize most in your life? Are there any material, personal, or societal influences you may be placing above God?

_____
_____
_____
_____
_____
_____
_____
_____
_____
_____
_____
_____

Why is it vital to surrender to the Lord?

_____
_____
_____
_____
_____
_____
_____
_____
_____
_____
_____

Listen for Insight and Instruction

James 1: 19-20 - *My dear brothers and sisters, take note of this: Everyone should be quick to listen, slow to speak, and slow to become angry. Human anger does not produce the righteousness that God desires.*

Ephesians 4:26-27 - *"In your anger do not sin": Do not let the sun go down while you are still angry, and do not give the devil a foothold.*

Instruction - a direction calling for compliance; order.

Lead with your ears. Before you can resolve the tension, you must first listen. This is the opposite of acting on feelings or sight. By leading with your ears, you allow your mind and heart to process what it has heard and often allow anger and unwanted reactions to dissolve. As a follower of Christ, it is necessary to submit your words and responses to the Lord. This includes not tossing responsibility onto others in anger and as a means to relinquish blame. Surrender to God as quickly and as much as needed to allow Him to work the anger out and release tensions. Resist the devil, and he will surely flee (James 4:7). Remember, he does not have authority over you or your situation. He is under you as well as your situation and without authorization, undeserving, and unworthy of what you have access to as a child of God. Learn to trust God with your thoughts before they come out as words that can not be erased. Learning to find resolutions to issues is a gift that is and can be empowered by the Lord.

Reflections

Where do you seek guidance intentionally to gain insight?

_____

_____

_____

_____

_____

_____

_____

_____

_____

_____

_____

What type of insight are you taking in now?

_____

_____

_____

_____

_____

_____

_____

_____

_____

_____

_____

Ways & Words of Wisdom

Hebrews 6:9-12 - *Even though we speak like this, dear friends, we are convinced of better things in your case—the things that have to do with salvation. God is not unjust; He will not forget your work and the love you have shown him as you have helped His people and continue to help them. We want each of you to show this same diligence to the very end, so that what you hope for may be fully realized. We do not want you to become lazy, but to imitate those who through faith and patience inherit what has been promised.*

Wisdom - ability to discern inner qualities and relationships: insight.

The Words of the Lord include good things being spoken over His children. He said in His Word that He wants His people to keep faith and help others. Doing so will result in a harvest to reap. Stick with it, do not give up; follow through (Revelations 14:12). God gave you His promise that His Word will never return back void because God is not a man that He should lie (Titus 1:2). He is an unchangeable Lord. You can always depend on Him and trust Him never to leave nor forsake you. As His own, His spirit lives in you. Teach yourself to speak the good things over and ahead of you, just as the Father did. Affirm and agree with the Lord in the great things He has rewarded you and all He has in store for your life.

Reflections

Write down the words you often say to yourself. Then, challenge yourself to become more aware of your self-talk daily—watch your words and speak life.

_____

_____

_____

_____

_____

_____

_____

_____

_____

_____

_____

What are examples of words of wisdom that the Bible offers to God's people?

_____

_____

_____

_____

_____

_____

_____

_____

_____

_____

_____

Distinguish Yourself Differently

Proverbs 31:10-31 - *A wife of noble character who can find? She is worth far more than rubies. Her husband has complete confidence in her and lacks nothing of value. She brings him good, not harm, all the days of her life. She selects wool and flax and works with eager hands. She is like the merchant ships, bringing her food from afar. She gets up while it is still night; she provides food for her family and portions for her female servants. She considers a field and buys it; out of her earnings she plants a vineyard. She sets about her work vigorously; her arms are strong for her tasks. She sees that her trading is profitable, and her lamp does not go out at night. In her hand she holds the distaff and grasps the spindle with her fingers. She opens her arms to the poor and extends her hands to the needy. When it snows, she has no fear for her household; for all of them are clothed in scarlet. She makes coverings for her bed; she is clothed in fine linen and purple. Her husband is respected at the city gate, where he takes his seat among the elders of the land. She makes linen garments, sells them, and supplies the merchants with sashes. She is clothed with strength and dignity; she can laugh at the days to come. She speaks with wisdom, and faithful instruction is on her tongue. She watches over the affairs of her household and does not eat the bread of idleness. Her children arise and call her blessed; her husband also, and he praises her: "Many women do noble things, but you surpass them all." Charm is deceptive, and beauty is fleeting; but a woman who fears the Lord is to be praised. Honor her for all that her hands have done, and let her works bring her praise at the city gate.*

Distinguish - to hear or see clearly; make out, discern (distinguish a light in the distance); to know or point out the difference (differentiate between right and wrong); to set apart as different or unique.

God has been drawing my attention to this scripture for years, speaking to me through it in ways I didn't fully understand at the time. I even received a bookmark with this verse on it, and I held on to it for years because it resonated deeply in my spirit. I sensed its significance would become clear one day at the right time. So I kept it in a special spot—hidden away so it wouldn't get lost but close enough to find if I felt led to it again. Occasionally, I would come across it, but on one particular day, as I turned into my neighborhood, I opened my sun visor, instinctively reached for it, and there it was. At that moment, God gave me the name *Beyond Measure.*

Beyond Measure is the name of my nonprofit organization and mentorship program, which is currently being established. As led by the Holy Spirit, I have mentored young girls, especially teen mothers, offering encouragement, support, and prayer to discern how to help them best. My mission is to provide resources, knowledge, and inspiration to help them navigate challenges that may feel overwhelming. By God's grace, I aim to empower them not to be defined by their circumstances but to rise beyond their expectations and limitations.

I know firsthand how it feels to lack self-belief and struggle with feelings of worthlessness—a weight no one should carry alone. If I can use my experiences to be open and honest, helping others rebuild their self-esteem, self-respect, and sense of worth, I will gladly serve as a vessel for God's glory. This is my calling: to walk alongside those in need and remind them that they can live a life *beyond measure with God.*

Prayerfully, these efforts will inspire others, as they did for me, to use the Bible as a guiding example in becoming the woman and wife we are called to be. This passage from Proverbs serves as both my reminder and my goal: to live in a way that pleases God.

Reflections

What do you need to discern more of?

_____
_____
_____
_____
_____
_____
_____
_____
_____

How are you different from those around you? What does this mean to the Lord?

_____
_____
_____
_____
_____
_____
_____
_____
_____
_____

Serve with Sincerity

Philippians 2:3-4, 14 - *Do nothing out of selfish ambition or vain conceit. Rather, in humility value others above yourselves, not looking to your own interests but each of you to the interests of the others. Do everything without grumbling or arguing*

Serve - to provide services that benefit or help.

What are your motives for helping others? If your answer is anything other than their benefit and well-being, it's time to reassess. Genuine service should humble your heart, not inflate your ego. When you extend a helping hand, it's essential to focus on others—their needs, preferences, and perspectives. Sometimes, serving means lifting others quietly without seeking recognition. Your heart must be aligned with the right intentions to serve willingly and without complaints or arguments. Pure motives are vital when serving both the Lord and others; otherwise, it's better not to serve at all (Deut. 28:47).

Serving may include lending a hand without expecting something in return. You may think this is not logical, but according to the Bible, you should help others without considering the investment return. Your sincere heart should lead with concern and care for others' best interests. Challenge yourself to help someone find a solution, whether to a spoken conflict, an internal issue, or a tangible situation. This is the way of the Lord's Son, Jesus, who lives in you and was sent as the only way to get you to Heaven.

Reflections

What are some opportunities to help others in your community/area?

_____
_____
_____
_____
_____
_____
_____
_____
_____
_____

In what ways can you ensure sincerity is shown in all you do for others?

_____
_____
_____
_____
_____
_____
_____
_____
_____
_____

Declare Demonstration

Isaiah 55:11 - *So is my word that goes out from my desire by the speech flowing from your mouth: It will not return to me empty, but will accomplish what I desire and achieve the purpose for which I sent it.*

Declare - *obsolete; to make clear; to make evident; show.*

Demonstrations - an outward expression or display.

You have power within you to declare and speak things into existence. This means you can call for things to be shown to you as evidence and proof of being done. The words of your mouth have lots of power alone. God's Holy power can go before you and demonstrate the Word of God just because you say it aloud. God is not a man, and He shall not lie. He will always have results. With Christ, you can accomplish what you desire by the speech flowing from your mouth. By getting comfortable with declaring things by faith, you are destined to succeed and have no choice but to witness God's glory. The Lord wants to produce demonstrations on your behalf, so you must speak confidently and by faith.

Reflections

How can you get in the habit of declaring evidence over your life?

_____

_____

_____

_____

_____

_____

_____

_____

_____

_____

List some things you believe in God for. Read them aloud daily.

_____

_____

_____

_____

_____

_____

_____

_____

_____

_____

Bask in Beautiful Blessings

Daniel 10:12 - *Then he continued, "Do not be afraid, Daniel. Since the first day you set your mind to gain understanding and humble yourself before your God, your words were heard, and I have responded to them."*

Bask - to lie or relax in a pleasant warmth or atmosphere.

Blessings - the act or words of one that blesses; approval, encouragement; a thing conducive to happiness or welfare; grace said at a meal.

Okay, God! *May He allow you to apologize for all the ways you choose against Him.* Whether it's not putting Him first, compromising your faith, or not fully trusting the Lord, tell God you apologize for almost canceling your blessings by being selfish and stressed. Let Him know you appreciate Him for still loving you and showing up in ways no one has ever done or could ever do for you. Look into your life; see the paths, people, places, or things that were all a part of His plan. He ordained most strategically for you to testify of God's goodness. You could have been dead and gone, making the choices that you have in the past. Instead, the Lord saw fit to use you and keep you around, so for that, you should be grateful.

Blessings are often inside you, waiting for you to activate them once they are accessed. Knowing your heart and God's heart is a gift and blessing to all His people to saturate their souls. When you pray, ask for acceptance, transparency, and humility, among many other things, so that you can say, "Yes, Lord, I understand." This, too, will remind you that He is hearing your prayers. God can bless you to enjoy and engage in the favor and level of blessings He leads you towards. With great honor for your purpose of obtaining the vision you know He has planned for you and gifted you with for others, the Lord is gracious and kind. It is ahead, so be ready for it! Let Him use you in life and reap the harvest that is the fruit of the Lord's hand on you as a good and faithful servant.

Reflections

What has grace and mercy done for you?

_____

_____

_____

_____

_____

_____

_____

_____

_____

_____

_____

Why is it Important to Recognize the Blessings of God?

_____

_____

_____

_____

_____

_____

_____

_____

_____

_____

Kenneidra Brown-Bender is a devoted wife, mother of two, and first-time author embarking on an impactful journey to inspire others through her faith-based writing. Her debut series, *Beyond Measure: Renewing Your Mind God's Way, Volume 1*, delves into the transformative power of aligning one's mind with God's principles, guiding readers toward spiritual renewal and growth. In addition to her writing, Kenneidra serves her community with compassion and dedication as part of the team at St. Clair Sav-A-Life. Her work there embodies her heart for helping others navigate challenging seasons with grace and hope, reflecting her commitment to family and faith-driven service. Kenneidra Brown-Bender is a devoted wife, mother of two, and first-time author embarking on an impactful journey to inspire others through her faith-based writing. Her debut series, Beyond Measure: Renewing Your Mind God's Way, Volume 1, delves into the transformative power of aligning one's mind with God's principles, guiding readers toward spiritual renewal and growth. In addition to her writing, Kenneidra serves her community with compassion and dedication as part of the Sav-a-Life Pregnancy Test Center team. Her work there embodies her heart for helping others navigate challenging seasons with grace and hope, reflecting her commitment to family and faith-driven service.

Connect With Me

I appreciate your interest in Beyond Measure and the transformative journey it offers. Whether you have questions about the devotional, want to share your story, or are seeking additional resources, we would love to hear from you.

Reach Out Today
Website: www.youarebeyondmeasure.org
Email: info@youarebeyondmeasure.org

Feel free to connect with us through our website or email for more information, to ask about upcoming events, or to explore how Beyond Measure can inspire your walk of faith. We look forward to walking alongside you as you discover a life of freedom and purpose!

References

Merriam-Webster. (2023, February 5). Clarity. Merriam-Webster.com Thesaurus. https://www.merriam-webster.com/thesaurus/clarity

Merriam-Webster. (2023, February 9). Humility. Merriam-Webster.com Thesaurus. https://www.merriam-webster.com/thesaurus/humility

Merriam-Webster. (2023, January 17). Mind. Merriam-Webster.com Dictionary. https://www.merriam-webster.com/dictionary/mind

Merriam-Webster. (2023, February 10). Obey. Merriam-Webster.com Thesaurus. https://www.merriam-webster.com/thesaurus/obey

Merriam-Webster. (2023, January 31). Perception. Merriam-Webster.com Dictionary. https://www.merriam-webster.com/dictionary/perception

Merriam-Webster. (2023, February 9). Pride. Merriam-Webster.com Thesaurus. https://www.merriam-webster.com/thesaurus/pride

Merriam-Webster. (2023, February 14). Rebuke. Merriam-Webster.com Dictionary. https://www.merriam-webster.com/dictionary/rebuke

Merriam-Webster. (2023, February 3). Transparency. Merriam-Webster.com Thesaurus. https://www.merriam-webster.com/thesaurus/transparency

Merriam-Webster. (2023, February 10). Trust. Merriam-Webster.com Thesaurus. https://www.merriam-webster.com/thesaurus/trust

Merriam-Webster. (2023, February 10). Worry. Merriam-Webster.com Dictionary. https://www.merriam-webster.com/dictionary/worry

Merriam-Webster. (2023, March 7). Access. Merriam-Webster.com Dictionary. https://www.merriam-webster.com/dictionary/access

Merriam-Webster. (2023, March 7). Understand. Merriam-Webster.com Dictionary. https://www.merriam-webster.com/dictionary/understand

Merriam-Webster. (2023, March 7). Transparent. Merriam-Webster.com Dictionary. https://www.merriam-webster.com/dictionary/transparent

Merriam-Webster. (2023, March 7). Accept. Merriam-Webster.com Dictionary. https://www.merriam-webster.com/dictionary/accept

Merriam-Webster. (2023, March 9). Toss. Merriam-Webster.com Dictionary. https://www.merriam-webster.com/dictionary/toss

Merriam-Webster. (2023, March 14). Release. Merriam-Webster.com Dictionary. https://www.merriam-webster.com/dictionary/release

Merriam-Webster. (2023, March 14). Trust. Merriam-Webster.com Dictionary. https://www.merriam-webster.com/dictionary/trust

Merriam-Webster. (2023, October 14). Doubt. Merriam-Webster.com Dictionary. https://www.merriam-webster.com/dictionary/doubt

Merriam-Webster. (2023, October 27). Renew. Merriam-Webster.com Dictionary. https://www.merriam-webster.com/dictionary/renew

Merriam-Webster. (2023, October 30). Force. Merriam-Webster.com Dictionary. https://www.merriam-webster.com/dictionary/force

Merriam-Webster. (2023, November 26). Purify. Merriam-Webster.com Dictionary. https://www.merriam-webster.com/dictionary/purify

Merriam-Webster. (2023, December 29). Extend. Merriam-Webster.com Dictionary. https://www.merriam-webster.com/dictionary/extend

Merriam-Webster. (2023, December 29). Grace. Merriam-Webster.com Dictionary. https://www.merriam-webster.com/dictionary/grace

Merriam-Webster. (2024, June 20). Manage. Merriam-Webster.com Dictionary. https://www.merriam-webster.com/dictionary/manage

Merriam-Webster. (2024, June 20). Discipline. Merriam-Webster.com Dictionary. https://www.merriam-webster.com/dictionary/discipline

Merriam-Webster. (2024, June 20). Positive. Merriam-Webster.com Dictionary. https://www.merriam-webster.com/dictionary/positive

Merriam-Webster. (2024, June 21). Power. Merriam-Webster.com Dictionary. https://www.merriam-webster.com/dictionary/power

Merriam-Webster. (2024, June 21). Speak. Merriam-Webster.com Dictionary. https://www.merriam-webster.com/dictionary/speak

Merriam-Webster. (2024, June 24). Profess. Merriam-Webster.com Dictionary. https://www.merriam-webster.com/dictionary/profess

Merriam-Webster. (2024, June 25). Believe. Merriam-Webster.com Dictionary. https://www.merriam-webster.com/dictionary/believe

Merriam-Webster. (2024, July 1). Persevere. Merriam-Webster.com Dictionary. https://www.merriam-webster.com/dictionary/persevere

www.ingramcontent.com/pod-product-compliance
Lightning Source LLC
Chambersburg PA
CBHW071532120626
46550CB00006B/2431